In Venice, around the 13th century, laws were passed restricting the use of masks. Henceforth, Venetians and foreign visitors, alike, were permitted to wear masks only during the days of carnival and at official banquets. These organised events, to which masks could be worn, were the beginnings of the Carnival of Venice.

An elaborate Venetian mask

Couples often attended as allegorical characters or in complementary costumes.

Masquerade balls, which were attended by guests in masked costumes, date back to late medieval European court life. In the15th century, masquerade balls become part of public festivities in Venice and other European cities. By the 16th and 17th centuries their popularity continued.

As the clown character of the Harlequin (dating from the 16th-century Italian theatre *Commedia dell'arte*) developed he also began wearing a mask. In fact, this was to become an intrinsic part of his costume.

Feathers have long adorned masks such as this domino-style mask.

Masks on sticks, which have been popular since masquerade balls began, enable the wearer to briefly reveal his or her identity to favoured dance partners.

Harlequin

The colourful diamond-patterned hat symbolises the Harlequin.

The Harlequin first appeared in a type of travelling street theatre called *Commedia dell'arte*, which originated in Italy in the 16th century. *Commedia* players performed a repertoire of stories that would have been familiar to their audiences. Each character was identified by costume.

The Harlequin (also known as Arlecchino) was a clown, traditionally played by a man dressed in shabby clothes patched with various colours. His pale powdered face was smeared with dirty marks.

As this character developed, so did the costume. The patches became colourful 'diamond-shaped' designs and the dirty marks on his face were replaced by a black mask.

A loose smock-style top with large ruffles and loose-fitting trousers decorated with colourful 'diamonds' and pompoms complete the part for this romantic version of the Harlequin.

Rich silk gives this clown's costume a glamorous edge.

Coppelia

Distinctively painted doll's cheeks are a feature of this mask.

Is she real or is she a doll? A mischievous role to play.

Coppelia, sub-titled *The girl with the enamel eyes*, is probably the best-known comedy ballet. Its premier in 1870 was attended by the leading figures of Parisian society, and was an immediate success. With its brightness, humour and vigorous national dances, it was a departure from the sad and romantic ballets of the day. The musical score was also gay and distinctive for the era, and the story had a happy ending.

Coppelia is a beautiful doll in a shop window in a small village. She seemingly comes to life, but actually a mischievous girl called Swanilda has taken the doll's place – fooling everyone.

Satin ballet shoes tied with ribbons complete the picture.

A colourful tutu trimmed with flowers and a simple black velvet choker is perfect for this costume.

Carmen

Red for passion, black for mystery and red roses for romance and love

Red roses and peinetas (ornate comb) feature on this mask.

Carmen, written by the French composer Georges Bizet, is set in 1830 in Seville, Spain. This opera premiered in 1875 at the Opera-Comique, Paris, but it was ahead of its time, and the audience jeered at it. Critics also denounced it at first. However, it has since become one of the world's most popular operas. The story, concerning a seductress, a soldier who breaks rank and a band of gypsies and thieves, was considered inappropriate in its day.

However, the story of Carmen, the beautiful, fiery Spanish gypsy, eventually captured audiences, as did Bizet's wonderful music.

This Spanish-influenced ensemble, with its corseted waistline, peasant blouse and layered gathered skirt – offset by a fringed scarf tied around the hips – is perfect for the passionate temptress. Such accessories as a lace fan and a fringed scarf are used for added allure.

Shoes made for Spanish dancing are worn for the part.